Red Army Red

Red Army Red

poems

JEHANNE DUBROW

TRIQUARTERLY BOOKS
NORTHWESTERN UNIVERSITY PRESS
EVANSTON, ILLINOIS

TriQuarterly Books
Northwestern University Press
www.nupress.northwestern.edu

Printed in the United States of America

10 9 8 7 6 5 4 3 2 1

Library of Congress Cataloging-in-Publication Data
Dubrow, Jehanne.
   Red army red : poems / Jehanne Dubrow.
     p. cm.
   Includes bibliographical references.
   ISBN 978-0-8101-2860-6 (pbk. : alk. paper)
   1. Adolescence—Poetry. 2. Americans—Europe, Eastern—Poetry. I. Title.
PS3604.U276R43 2012
811.6—dc23

                                             2012011871

SUSTAINABLE FORESTRY INITIATIVE

Certified Sourcing
www.sfiprogram.org
SFI-01234

CONTENTS

laissez-faire

ACKNOWLEDGMENTS

Barn Owl Review: "Wiretap"

Blackbird: "In the Grand Theater," "Iron Curtain," "Purged History Of," and "Three Generations"

Cave Wall: "November 1989" and "The Russian Ballerina"

Cerise Press: "A Small History of Shopping"

Cincinnati Review: "Five-Year Plan"

Connecticut River Review: "Notes from the City of Revolution"

Diode: "Grunge" and "Water Through a Hand"

Linebreak: "Eastern Bloc"

Mid American Review: "Before Pleasure"

New Republic: "Tea"

Pleiades: "Moscow Nights"

Ploughshares: "The Crowd in the City Square"

Prairie Schooner: "Fancy," "Our Free-Market Romance," "Puberty, as Poem by Akhmatova," and "Velvet Revolution"

Raintown Review: "Bribes My Family Made"

Rattle: "The Cold War, a Romance" and "Nowa Huta"

Southwest Review: "Agora"

Vinyl Poetry: "As Seen on TV," "Just Say No," and "Vinegar Aphrodisiac"

West Branch: "Aubade" and "Chernobyl Year"

"Chernobyl Year" was featured as a newspaper column (no. 320) in Ted Kooser's American Life in Poetry project.

"Chernobyl Year," "Eastern Bloc," and "Tea" were reprinted as broadsides for the exhibit "Poetic Aesthetic" at the University of Maryland, with artwork by Tim Gough.

I am extremely grateful for the support of the Sewanee Writers' Conference, the West Chester University Poetry Conference, and Washington College.

A number of texts became my companions during the writing of this collection, including Svetlana Alexievich's *Voices from Chernobyl,* Timothy Garton Ash's *The Magic Lantern* and *The Polish Revolution,* Simon Schama's *Landscape and Memory,* and Charity Scribner's *Requiem for Communism.* I also relied on Lawrence Weschler's "The Graphics of Solidarity," which first appeared in an issue of *The Virginia Quarterly Review.*

Thank you to the people who encouraged me with long conversations about All Things Poetry, lunches at Brooks Tavern, or other necessary forms of counsel: Sandra Beasley, Kim Bridgford, Claudia Emerson, Jennifer Hansen, Leslie Harrison, Robert Hass, Erika Meitner, Kristin Naca, and Yerra Sugarman. Many thanks to my editor at Northwestern University Press, Mike Levine. An extra special *thank-you* to Meredith Hadaway, my weekly writing partner, who saw most of these poems in their greenest shapes.

Finally, my love and gratitude to my mother, Jeannette (press agent extraordinaire); to my father, Steve; to my brother, The Schmer; and to Argos the WonderPup.

And to Jeremy, who remains the other half of this nation-of-two.

Red Army Red

Chernobyl Year

We dreamed of glowing children,
their throats alive and cancerous,
their eyes like lightning in the dark.

We were uneasy in our skins,
sixth grade, a year for blowing up,
for learning that nothing contains

that heat which comes from growing,
the way our parents seemed at once
both tall as cooling towers and crushed

beneath the pressure of small things—
family dinners, the evening news,
the dead voice of the dial tone.

Even the ground was ticking.
The parts that grew grew poison.
Whatever we ate became a stone.

Whatever we said was love became
plutonium, became a spark
of panic in the buried world.

cold war

Moscow Nights

Praise rose perfume
that smells of piss.

Praise the shop girl,
spraying a wrist

with pickled beets
and turpentine.

Praise ambergris
formaldehyde.

Praise the bottle
sickled gold,

its stopper fatter
than a comrade's fist.

Praise the Communist.
Praise musk, the deer

that gives up
greases from its glands.

Praise the mermaid,
herring mist,

oyster shell,
pearl of mucus

dreaming in its bed.
Praise the customer,

who dabs her pulse
with chicken fat.

Praise dead bouquets
beside the grave.

And praise the grave
itself, the dirt

a fixative,
the wood an incense

to an iron church,
the burning scent of snow.

Aubade

Often I lay awake to listen for
my parents returning from the embassy,
a key toothing the lock, the front door

opening to let them in, its rusty
hinges a metal warning. Every
evening the same. I drank the words *cold war*

from the water glass on my nightstand.
I watched the clock hands glow or spoke into
my pillow, tapped out minutes with my hand.

Sometimes my parents missed the curfew.
Trapped at work, they slept on couches, made do
with a dinner of saltines. They never planned

to stay so late, much less to watch the sky
from their offices, the night beginning gray
then turned to carbon paper. I can't deny

the imprint of their absence, the way
my room was shadow and the ricochet
of light, hard sheets, green hours ticking by.

Vinegar Aphrodisiac

> People said back then that there was only vinegar in the
> stores. It obviously turned out to be a powerful aphrodisiac
> since it led to the birth of 14 million new Poles.
> —WOJCIECH JARUZELSKI, FORMER DICTATOR

I want you most as raveled socks. I want
     you car, you Fiat and Trabant

that take the street on wobble-wheels, all spit
     and sputter. You plate without meat,

you Warsaw Zoo without its elephant,
     Swan Lake without Odette. In fact,

no swan in the aviary of your heart.
     No hammered beak. How long I wait

to hear No bread, No toilet paper, No sugar
     for a week. I buy you pickle jar.

I subsidize you cabbage in the fall.
     I eat you in my stew. You sell

for forty dollars on the black market.
     When you are denim counterfeit,

I like how close you fit against my hips.
     Old heroes may be dead, shops

gone, but you are still a marble bust
        that pigeons leave alone. Mostly.

You're still the news on all two channels.
        How well they read your name. And still

red currants in a bowl. Who cares about
        the sour juice of you? What's sweet

without the wanting, the queue around the block
        when even you are out of stock?

Fancy

Those evenings when they dressed for an affair,
    my parents were most beautiful, my father stiff,
so sensitive to the strip of silk around his throat
    that he barely moved, except to hold the door
for my mother, and my mother's neck a naked
    thing above her gown, the bow that rustled
when she stood, like a satin orchid planted near
    her skin. Her shoes were thin, sharp knives,
making a sound I knew as fancy, *click-clack*
    click-clack across the black-and-white foyer.
They pinched her toes, she said, which was her way
    of telling me that loveliness should hurt. Even
before she left, her hair loosened from its bun,
    as though something in her wanted to escape.

    I rarely heard them coming home after the waltz
and gin, ungloved, unfastened from the car,
    his hand resting on the small secret of her back,
her zipper finally splitting at the teeth. But I
    imagined them speaking French or Polish at a party,
holding the words so long inside their mouths
    that language felt like infidelity, made me look
away. Each morning my mother's velvet purse
    wilted on a chair, empty of its midnight contents:
ruby lipstick, tiny lake of a pocket mirror.
    My father's tie lay crumpled on the bed.
The romance of objects—both their costumes
    on hangers again, still clasping the scent
of two bodies that bent, unbent inside of them.

Purged History Of

After Janice R. Harrington

and hookers wore their hair red army red
a Decalogue of reddened fingernails

red-hot brassieres red nipples underneath
red welts where customers had stroked too hard

and later they sweated in the afterglow
of red smoked cigarettes whose embers sparked

the dark a cherry-red their pillows propped
red dreams and workers stood in line to buy

red books and read red pages on the tram
to work each creed a monolith of red

each stop another passage through the red
that dyed December on May Day they sang red

their children marched in red parades behind
a convoy of red tanks the wind blew red

because the leaves could only leave the branch
as different shades of mandatory red

and all the maps were demarcated red
the red of flags of blood on cinder blocks

and wire shelves gaped empty in the stores
except for red in three varieties

and 1 + 1 would always equal red
and red the baby's name first word first step

the scarlet fever when the pills ran out
the mouth that swallowed every cure for red

Bribes My Family Made

for seven pairs of jeans you get a maid
for information you get sex   for sex
six cigarettes a can of caviar
for comic books a flask of French perfume

for information you get sex   for sex
you get a Polish ham a handyman
for Superman a flacon of French perfume
a hand grenade   and dollar bills will buy

a Polish ham a Polish handyman
a one-way limousine to West Berlin
a hand job on the way   or dollars buy
your pick of concerts at the Opera House

no questions   gets you straight to West Berlin
for peep shows on the dirty side of town
you get the front row at the Opera House
a magnum of our finest pink champagne

for peep shows topless dancers   XXX
you get your passport and your visa stamped
this magnum of our finest pink champagne
can ship your favorite secret to the States

you get your passport and your visa stamped
for cigarettes   six cans of caviar
can get one secret smuggled to the States
for seven maids you get a pair of jeans

Photograph of My Father with Lech Wałęsa

As far as compositions go,
it isn't art—my father on the left,
Wałęsa standing square,

stolid in the frame
like concrete poured into
the shape of someone eminent,

and on the right, a guy
we can't remember anymore,
midlevel civil servant,

no doubt useful in his time.
All three lapels are pinned
with flags or pictures

of the Black Madonna,
white shirts green beneath
the bureaucratic light,

the end of the decade propped
on padded shoulders.
One year from here,

Wałęsa will be president.
Perhaps, he's staring
at the future now, dark

pinpoint against the lens.
On either side of him:
teeth, the switched-on smiles

of Americans. It's always like this,
the famous and the not
and somewhere beside

the two, my father
turning from the camera
to grin at history in the middle,

or glancing at the other guy,
charcoal suit of anonymity,
already trying to recall a name.

At the 600-Year-Old Restaurant

Wierzynek Restaurant in Kraków

Imagine centuries of lunch,
centuries of the busboy's doublet
stained with mead martinis,
today's special a trencher
of boar, the iron chandelier
a prop from the Inquisition.
And later, eras of cabbage
in all its folded varieties.
One hundred years of juniper.
The Age of Buttermilk.
When Sweden attacks, the chef
learns how to bury fish to cure
the flesh. After the Russians,
dumplings grow heavy
with sadness, drown in sauce.
The city burns from old to new.
But here, patrons eat pebbles
of dough, soup from the nothing
of pickle juice. Everything
is egg or shortages of egg,
everything the bottom
of the bowl, the apple peel.
Someone changes a tablecloth.
Someone lights a taper on
the modern condition, which
seems familiar as half-chewed
bread or a plate of reheated meat.

Nowa Huta

"New Steelworks," the socialist realist city

In the model city, nothing seems to work, not the winch, the derrick, the coal-dust men, not the foreman shouting *Get up, boys, go work.*

Our philosophy was made to work—chug chug the sleek machine, the chiseled men of the model city. Everything seemed to work

at first. Remember how the children worked at doing sums? The wives at pleasing men? The foreman shouting *Get up, boys, go work?*

Even the sun was busy with its work of shining gold on all the marble men. Now in the model city, nothing seems to work.

The brick is crumbling, and the stonework turns to powder under hand. The men ignore the foreman who's shouting *work,*

you cogwheels, work. Goddamn this heavy work we bang our heads against. Goddamn the men, the model city, where nothing comes of work. To hell the foreman shouting *workworkwork.*

Three Generations

Oil painting, Jerzy Duda-Gracz, 1989

Here, we see the crooked house
in a listing countryside, Poland
of mud, roads furrowed as a brow,
falling-down fences. Grandma
is stooped by the weight of a lumpy
sky. Arthritic knuckles, pebbles
for knees. Beside her, a middle-aged
daughter, skin the color of walked-
on snow except for her scraped cheeks.
And between them both, a little girl
wearing the dull blue that can only
mean winter. In this world, women
are old and fat, or else they're thin
wire, their faces molded clay. But
what we remember most is the shawl
one of them wears on her shoulders,
fabric patterned like a tired field,
pink roses done with blossoming.

The Crowd in the City Square

has become one knotted rope
one breath of cabbage soup

one foot on the cobblestone—
a thousand banners—no—one

flag flapping its red letters
into a satin tatter

because this is the century
of slivers and scraps—beauty

of the dustbin—the crowd knows
that nothing good can follow

from that other prettiness
—the slick summer palaces

of the tyrant—the mansions
iced like cakes for children—

the crowd wears a glove with holes
worn in the fingertips and pulls

at a thread—the crowd loses
all feeling in its thin nose—

so lovely to be shattered
not far from the granite stairs

and the tinkling chandelier
in the city of nowhere—

the city of discarded
ironies—lost shoes and scarves

The Russian Ballerina

As if some trick of the theater,
                    she fluttered from the stage to curl
her body on our couch, feathers pulled
          from the dark fist of her hair.

Everywhere we looked, she was thin
                    as tulle, clavicle of glass,
her limbs designed for arabesque,
          one leg stretched back, one straight-pinned

to the floor. What longing was:
                    a pas de deux between the dancer and
herself. Even at dinner, her hands
          kept whispering from pose to pose.

Fingers of Grief. Palm of Absence.
                    And her feet—no longer sewn
with ribbon, the tiny, wrenched bones—
          were almost birds from a distance.

The Cold War, a Romance

Sometimes we were illegal dollar bills.
We were the three-hour line for bread,
    the last pair of panty hose in the shop,
the hard potato. Or else, we were the town
    of industry where all machines had stopped,
the stalled assembly line, the pneumatic drills.
    We were the wiretap, the rumor spread
from room to room. We were the State crackdown.
    And yes, we were the act of making do—
a soup of water, salt, one chicken bone.
    We were vodka swigged against the chill,
and the sad folk song that every soldier knew,
    and the ribbon in the yellow hair, and the stone
that signified bodies on the hill.

Notes from the City of Revolution

At the shipyard, the workers went on strike again. This time, the artist drew a portrait of the union leader—walrus mustache, iron hands, neck a piece of welded pipe. A journalist wired the story to the press. A photographer shot the speeches through the wire fence. The air was made of wire and electricity. Soon half the city lost its electricity. Soon half the city lost its loaf of bread. On stage the actor said, The cost of milk can turn a country white. The cost of pills can march the army out. Shut yourself in. Prepare for the longest winter. Then came martial law, a city under curfew like a teenage girl. All doors locked. Nothing left to do but flirt in back rooms, share cigarettes, print pamphlets on the creaking press. Students groped in hallways of the university. They kissed against a tile stove. They were matches striking flint. This is the end of the world, they murmured in the burning of the other's body. There was nothing to do but write poetry. There was nothing to do but dream of chocolate, of Spain, of roses in the garden. At the embassy, even the chocolate had run out, diplomacy the taste of coal dust. The freeze is coming, a deputy announced. No one is listening, the poet sighed. He packed his bag to go. There was nowhere else to go. At the border, the suitcases were bricks that made a wall. And all the walls were visible—the columns in the paper shouting Solidarity, the old wars between lovers, the dead orchard where the apple tree still stands. Soon winter. And the belly groaned. Soon winter was the line, people waiting for kilo bags of sugar. They sweetened their tea with the memory of sugar. They closed their eyes against the soot. They tilted back their heads. Somehow they almost drank the honey of their tongues.

Crossing the Vistula

Early mornings. I was the only child on the school bus,

black rows of seats so empty that I tried to fill them

with my coat, scattered gloves like a pair of misplaced hands.

Warsaw's sky was low in winter, the sun white shadow

in sleet or snow. The driver turned up the radio

so that I could learn the sound of longing in the slow piano

which seemed to play all year. *Chopin,* he said. *Paderewski.*

And I could hear that being Polish was a field of hardened mud

and too many footprints, something foreign always

buried there. Always we crossed the bridge above the Vistula.

Everything I could say about that time was *always:*

pastries named for the buds of flowers, bouquets with odd

numbers of stems, never twelve but eleven, thirteen.

Always the first one on, the last one off. And books—

Little House on the Prairie, Little Women, A Little Princess

—all those tiny cities in my bag. This way of being

in a place before the streets have woken up,

only the movement of bakers and buses, of passing through

like water, the glide and tumble of December crows.

velvet revolution

Five-Year Plan

Like the Soviets, my body had a plan
   for every phase of development.
First hair in places where it wasn't meant
    to grow, bramble covering the compound.
Then curves like water waiting for a dam.
   Then electricity. And worse, a slight
atomic humming in my underground,
    the pulse of something nuclear all night—
adolescence, a make of tyranny
   I couldn't stand against. What to cut back?
What to prune or hack into obedience?
   My coal and oil, my machinery,
too much heat for my requirements,
   all production speeding out of whack.

Velvet Revolution

If she said I'm lonely,
her words were a curtain
over the dark of it.
And so she barely spoke.

Better to hold the peach,
not eating it, than feel
a pit against her teeth.
Apricots, plums, cherries,

all fruit reduced to stone,
like the mythology
of girls who discover
the wound of growing up.

When she rubbed the new hair,
there was a mutiny
called sex, a violence like
the riot that she'd seen

on the nightly news—
this pile and nap, this fur,
this violet murmuring
that knocked awake the blood.

In the Grand Theater

Five Decembers, I saw *Hänsel und Gretel* sung
by a pair of grown-up girls. And I waited

for the scene when trees began their flickering,
a thousand lightbulbs set to blink like fireflies.

Brother held sister's hand. Their voices
were melted chocolate and something else.

A knife. Then the woods unwrapped a candy house
where everything looked like toothache—

spun-sugar windows, gumdrop walls, an entrance
of black licorice. Then the cage. The finger

made of twigs to prove how thin the body is.
Raisins and almonds for stuffing,

the treble, like brittle in their baby-fat mouths.
I never expected them to escape each time,

blowing up the pulled-taffy roof with a fit
of strobes that always made me cry, twitch

in my red velvet dress. What I didn't know:
most stories involve devouring,

a duet of children at the witch's door
who watch gingerbread scorch in the oven,

or are eaten up by wolves, crumbs swallowed
somewhere on a raked and amber stage.

Wiretap

Poland, 1987

Two girls with the receivers pressed like shells against their ears, each voice the other's ocean. And in between the spilling out of words, the click-click-click of a machine recording all their treasures—coral lips they wore in school, the boy with azure eyes. Once, they misheard the term as *watertap*—speech a liquid thing to be turned on or off again. Somewhere there was a room of secrets: pierced ears, the kisses made with tongues that move like minnows, silvery and fast. The Hush-Hush room. The Confidence. Somewhere an index card with every name for azure eyes—they called him sea-glass boy, they called him Baltic Sea and jellyfish, they called him Sky Is Always Blue. All those longings larger than blue eyes, larger even than the body, which takes so long to find its shape, solidify to something heavier than water—and always then the scratch of pen on paper, soft as writing in the sand.

At the American School of Warsaw

Let the new class
proclaim the cafeteria
as their domain.

All spheres are theirs—
the lunch lady's slotted spoon,
the mashed potato lumps.

Even the apples
sweating on plastic trays
belong to them. Let

fluorescent lights shine on
the usual cruelty.
Dissected frogs, fetal pigs.

Let the new class replace
the old, Ambers
supplanting Britneys,

the way some swap
pink nails for redder ones.
Let them part

their hair along the right.
Soprano voices clang,
like the bells at 3:15.

Let the boys form rows
of footprints
on the wet linoleum,

lockers slamming shut,
a metal laughter
in the antiseptic air.

November 1989

I locked the bathroom door, spent hours
with a razor learning not to cut my legs,
powdering my arms to change the smell.
Outside our house: Warsaw, avenues
named for generals, poets from a partitioned
century. Everything was falling down.
The stone monument with its collapsing nose.
The wall that cut Berlin into a figure
and its sad reflection. I kept knocking
over furniture, as though someone
had moved the chairs. The days declared
themselves through silk drapes. Yellow
meant early morning. White was winter
dark. When it snowed, my parents called
history an unexpected guest who rings
the bell. *It's here,* they said and sang
"100 years" as Poles do to celebrate a birth.
They drank so many glasses of champagne.
Cocktail parties never stopped their crystal
clink or slurp of caviar. How small
my dresses hanging in the closet. Pink lace.
Lettuce-leaf hems. Pearl buttons down the back.
The news was chunked concrete, open
checkpoints, fingers making V for victory.
When it snowed, the city was clean amnesia,
the bullet holes from that other war
frosted over, faces of buildings gone blank,
the whole world trying not to bleed,
barely knowing itself in the mirror.

Puberty, as Poem by Akhmatova

The scarcity of milk—
that was me, and the queue
for a new pair of shoes.

I was the Russian verse
of frozen feet, the worst
winter in memory.

I was snowfall left piled
on New World Street. I was
boots that walked me black.

In the year of the long
freeze, other girls became
warm countries, while I stayed

behind, watched the dark parade
of seasons, waiting for
that one intemperate thing.

Martin

Martin by the lockers. Martin
       folding notes that held
my name, wrote *beautiful today,*
         a ballpoint portrait of my face.
Martin with an accent, the taste
        of smoke and juniper.
Martin smart, last one picked to play.
       Martin picked on
near the swerving of the swing.
        Martin made afraid of rope
and jungle gym. Tag,
        for Martin, the work of boys
who strike what's porcelain.
        Black-eyed Martin
with a black eye like a pencil smudge.
        Forgive me—I never hurt
the others for their game
        Kill Martin with the teacher's chalk.
All seventh grade the accident of pain.
        Martin asking for the slow
dance in the basement dark.
        His fingers left my back
so lonely when the music stopped.
        Martin with a box
of chocolate hearts. Martin
        liver-sick. No more not
kissing him, no more not
        looking when he offered
half a sandwich during lunch.

The empty seat where Martin
should have sat. Martin's
　　　bruise-turned-yellow skin.
The absence made of Martin,
　　　a word written, then erased.

Undergarments of the Soviet Era

They were the pair of rockets pointing West,
        a hook-and-eye defense against the pert
weapons of democracy. They propped each breast
                with starch and molded cups at Red Alert.
They were the corset laced enough to shield
        plutonium. Or bulletproof. Or thick
as a concrete Wall, a country sealed.
                They only came in fallout and Sputnik.
Like armored tanks, they only came in shades
        of camouflage. No pinks or violets.
No satin openings, but hard parades
             of polyester panties, pantalettes
that snagged at skin, ballistic garter belts,
        the girdles leaving autocratic welts.

Iron Curtain

Warsaw, Poland, 1988.
Three Minutes in the Closet meant

another stab
at learning how to kiss,

wire hangers clanging,
a pair of gray galoshes

knocked across the floor.
Pressed between

wool overcoats and winter
scarves, I smelled

the boy's cologne,
like something furred

had died inside his shirt.
Our teeth scraped together,

the friction of a car
that drags its muffler down

the road, his hands searching
the back pocket of my jeans

as though to find a missing key.
He whispered Polish phrases

in my neck, *your neck* he said
        your neck. I wanted words

that came out hot, American,
        like *kiss me fuck me fuck me.*

        I only tasted metal.
Or maybe I wanted to pull back

        the screen dividing us,
touch the velvet part of him,

break the skin's barrier,
        inflexible and cold.

A Samizdat History of the Body

First, on the back
of a napkin: a breast
        kissed with gravy
from a poet's lunch.
        Next, a clavicle taped
to a light post. Ten
        people touched the bone
before the police could
        tear it. Then a pair
of ankles printed on
        onion skin. It matters
that the ink was blue.
        And stolen.
One knuckle sprayed
        near government.
Not quite a fist but almost.
        Two eyes in the envelope's
tight crease. A nose.
        A torn document, elbows
hard pencil leads.
        A wire hair tied
to a prisoner's door.
        A knee in the camera.
At last, a spine inside
        the marching song.
A spine on every
        mimeograph machine.
The body warm
        with printing, wet
with all its furtive parts.

Tea

Tonight I'm fruit and clove. I'm bergamot.
I drop a teabag in the cup and boil
the kettle until it sings. As if on cue,
a part of me remembers how to brew
the darker things—those years I was a pot
of smoky leaves scented with orange oil.
Truth is: I don't remember much of school,
the crushed-up taste of it. I was a drink
forgotten on the table, left to cool.
I was a rusted tin marked *childhood*.
I don't remember wanting to be good
or bad, but only that I used to sink
in water and wait for something to unfurl,
the scent of summer in the jasmine pearl.

Romance, as Martial Law

We learned to love each other
by watching our parents
sneak dissidents from the city.

Remember the painter
who married oil to pigment—
our mothers helped him flee

with only brushes made of fur,
a few wet canvases. They sent
him wrapped in twine to Italy.

Our fathers touched the border
for small places of dissent,
fingernails of electricity

along the barbed wire.
We learned that love was reticent,
like the poet left empty

of all words; was under
cover, a blank apartment
where warm bodies used to be.

Eastern Bloc

The stores ran out of butter every day.
So you ran out, escaped your parents' house,

the crystal vases and the crystal bowls
of caviar. You were crystal too,

but hollow and ringing to the finger's touch.
Around the corner, you heard a polonaise

pushed from the lungs of some winded instrument.
The sky was soot, or else beet soup. So sour

you bought the one limp pastry at the bakery,
your mouth stuck shut with rose-petal jam.

You dreamed of warmth though you were always cold.
You dreamed of fleeing west, of white cities

where the word for hunger had ten synonyms,
and desire was a shopping cart to wheel

across the marble floor. And everything
an open hand promising to be filled.

laissez-faire

Bag 'N Save

Nobody knows if it is night or day
inside the Bag 'N Save. We walk the aisles
of twenty kinds of paper towels, the display
of Reynolds plastic wrap, the perfect smiles
that gleam from every tube of Crest. We're lost.
We lose our families near the razor blades.
We lose ourselves watching a steak defrost
within the deli case, how it turns a shade
of dying in the man-made light. Such thirst.
We want to shop and eat. We want to stuff
ourselves like Ziploc bags about to burst.
We want to be a box of Cocoa Puffs
or Cap'n Crunch. So this is paradise—
to be on sale among the merchandise.

Our Free-Market Romance

        is your debit card
inside the ATM of me
        is dollars spitting from a slot
the paper slap
        of a receipt
is you the shopping bag
        and me the whisper
of paisley-patterned silk
        is beaucoup bucks
cashmere to the touch
        is your new-car smell
my luxury of leather seats
        is cruise control
is interest-free
        is the sticky spot
where price tags used to be
        is costume jewelry
is the big box store
        the box of plastic things
that cost five cents
        is Made in China
bedsheets from Peru
        is china plates
is transport to the States
        is the yield our bodies
can produce
        is our bargain-
basement selves
        is the knotted pair
of us like shoes

52

       is the pair of skinny jeans
our laissez-faire
       is the green perfume
of money making
       money everywhere

Puberty, as the Character of Gordon Gekko

Wall Street (1987)

Greed was good, and I
was wingtipped and diversified.

I had a lot to teach you, pal,
about the way ambition ticks

inside of us, how it rises like a stock
then bottoms out.

I clipped the caps of big cigars.
I sold while things were hot.

Who fucked with me was fucked.
Kid, buddy, schmuck—I was the art

of war, if war was suspenders
and a shark-blue shirt.

I was the fat portfolio, fat wad
of bills, vein of fat in a slab of beef.

Greed was good. And I
was a Maserati driven off a cliff.

Just Say No

We all wore T-shirts that matched the White House lawn,

grass so green it looked like a music video.

When the First Lady arrived, we stood at the same time—

in unison, our teacher called it—as we had practiced

all that week. Nancy Reagan wore her usual shoulder pads.

My best friend Reese ate Reese's Pieces, pretending

they were pills, first browns then yellows and oranges.

We all held green balloons—aloft, our teacher said,

which meant up high. There were some words about

peer pressure and children's futures precious as a string

of pearls. An eighth grader read a poem about powder.

We all said no to horse and Mary Jane. Jenna Goodwin

let go of her balloon. Too soon, our teacher said.

A girl from Blessed Sacrament threw up her lunch.

And a boy from Murch—who knew about such things—

untied the latex opening of his balloon and gulped

at helium, his voice diluted cloud, floating away.

Agora

Permanent installation in Grant Park, Chicago
Magdalena Abakanowicz, 2006

Because every crowd at times
seems cast in iron, a roughly human
shape repeated, these nine-foot figures
don't so much surprise as reassure:
this is the city. As if by agreement,
they lumber about while standing still.
Some are turning toward the park,
and others face the street. Except,
above the chest there is no neck,
no face for facing anywhere.
We might say they've lost their heads.
The Polish artist and her assistants
polished each by hand, some bodies
modeled on the surfaces of bark
and others mottled fruit. If this
were a photograph or a sketch
of a mob scene, we would miss
how small the installation makes
us feel, just as citizens must have felt
when standing beneath the marble
colonnades in ancient Greece,
columns like sequences of soldiers
or long tallies of the dead. Indeed,
the artist (we learn from her statement)
has molded *the countless* in metal
or clay, the public square of history,
where a throng can shift from politics
to shopping to the sharpened end

of a flagpole. All forms are rooted
in concrete. Some sink. Others
try lifting metal feet to walk away.
Standing among them it's clear
we're much the same—three-dimensional
from the front, and from behind
the dark relief of hollowed trees.

Grunge

Ugly is the new beautiful, my best friend said,
        brushing shadow
on my eyes, a color called *sludge.*
        Suddenly plaid flannel
was a way of softening how strange we'd become,
        our arms like streets
in a stretched-out city, how tall we were,
        jangled with caffeine.
The end of school was a rest stop someone kept moving
        further away.
The clock kept dragging its aluminum hands.
        We changed our minds
about boys, dumped the ones who slid the walls
        of empty swimming pools,
gliding their skateboards in reverse.
        Or the debate champions
who answered every question with a rough
        tongue of tweed.
Other strangers were the answer. We tied
        on weighted boots,
painted our nails *radioactive,*
        forgot to wash
our hair. We played the same CD a thousand times,
        imagined heroin, cocaine,
any foreign beating in the blood. Ugly
        was the new desiring—
it made asphalt easy to love, our mouths a shade
        of *oil slick.*

River Phoenix

Somewhere you're still alive
outside the Viper Room.

And maybe getting old
is what you are, round

around the middle, cracking
beers with Kurt Cobain,

both of you still slouched
in perpetuity,

movie star and rock star,
still beautiful in the vein

of neglected instruments
leaned up against a wall.

And perhaps you're analog
in a discontinuous world,

still baring your collarbone
to the midnight audience

that has trouble sleeping.
And while the rest of us leave

our twenties the way we leave
cities for suburbia—

because what else is there?
—you're still following

the rumor of a body past
train tracks to the river

                of your name.

Water Through a Hand

In the changing room,
    a woman loops the tape
        around my chest.

I hold my breath against
    the measurement
        and remember

my mother, how she used
    to stand this close
        when I was five,

shampooing my hair,
    the scent of apples
        filling up our bath,

how I watched through wet
    eyelashes the small wet
        curls of her,

and her breasts that swayed
    like an afterthought
        of the body.

I never asked to touch,
    although I often did
        as if by accident.

At other times, so distant
　　from the nakedness
　　　　of the shower,

she exchanged a black lace bra
　　for nude, her back to me,
　　　　a strand of pearls

laid out across the bed,
　　her clip-on earrings
　　　　oystered in a velvet box.

That was thirty years ago,
　　when what I wanted
　　　　was dresses pink

as tender parts, or a pair
　　of Mary Janes
　　　　in mirror-shine. Here,

I raise my arms to learn
　　cup size and band.
　　　　I try on bits of cloth

that match my skin—
　　and this satin
　　　　paradox of women,

the wire of our movements,
　　the way we slip
　　　　like water through a hand.

Bad Romance

I hand my debit card to the cashier—two hundred fifty for a pair of pants. Somewhere the shelves are empty, but not here.

And then it's on to perfume, boutique beer, a buy-one special on the potted plants. I hand my MasterCard to the cashier.

And look! Black Spanx to elevate my rear, a Wonderbra to boost without implants. Somewhere the shelves are empty. But here

there's counterfeit Fendi and fake cashmere on sale (my kingdom for a cash advance). I hand my Diners Club to the cashier.

What next? A phone that fits inside my ear, a sixty-dollar candle made in France. Somewhere the shelves are empty, but not here.

I'm lost again in Muzak. All I hear is Lady Gaga singing "Bad Romance." I hand my AmEx Gold to the cashier. Somewhere the shelves are empty. Never here.

Russian Red

Lipstick made by M·A·C Cosmetics

When you are writing
    a book about Russians
        and the red of winter hands,

not to mention beet soup,
    and certain parts of the body,
        everything takes on the shade

of your poems. Your car is red,
    the steak you ate for lunch.
        The wallet you bought

at Bloomingdale's
    is just reiteration of the theme.
        No surprise, perhaps,

that the tube of lipstick—
    resembling more projectile
        or ballpoint pen

—sits so nicely in your hand.
    The sales associate
        shows how to pencil

your lips with nude,
    a hypernakedness like
        a clean piece of paper,

before swiping
    the real color across your lips.
        How red they look.

And the bluish undertone
    of the makeup
        makes your teeth whiter.

You wanted to seem French.
    But your mouth declares
        its independence.

This thing you are writing,
    it says, is garish and beautiful
        and bullet-shaped.

eBay Item: Number 360236731935

"Rare political pin, circa 1980"

So disposable, you thought nothing
of tacking dozens to your clothing,

your body a billboard, buttons
etched with anchors, pickets of iron

and steel. Those were years of rallies,
when broadsides nailed to walls

were a way of sending out reports.
T-shirts worn beneath other shirts

said something loud and muted,
like shouting *strike* in a padded room.

People went to jail for drawing pictures.
People went to jail for _____.

Today, for a starting bid of ten dollars,
you can own a piece of it once more:

how young you were inside the din
of history, how you would hold it again,

that flag (only a little chipped), red
enamel on a distant, metal field.

Warsaw IKEA

With apologies to W. H. Auden

About shopping they are never wrong, the new
Poles; how well they understand
the FINTORP baskets and BILLY bookshelves; how these replace
buying butter from the State or black-marketeering or just standing in a queue;
how, when the young are passionately waiting
at the checkout to pay for KLAPPSTA chairs, there always must be
the old guard, berating
Warsaw for its steel suspension bridge and planned
communities: they can recall
the appealing gray of cinder block,
pockmarked, heroic plaques unscrewed from walls,
kiosks that still stock
Russian cigarettes and coffee.

In IKEA, for instance: how everyone turns toward the display
of RÖNÅS candlesticks; the DOKUMENT letter tray
is also on sale, and why
not spring for a set of SLITBAR knives; the lights shine
as they have to on white counters in green
kitchens; and the STABIL splatter screen
will fit most frying pans, and each amazing buy,
ALMSTED and SKYN, BESTÅ and RODD, can be found in aisles 1 through 29.

A Small History of Shopping

When I was thirteen,
    my one-buck allowance
would buy a week

of luxury in Warsaw's shops,
    black-market leather,
amber chunks on silver chains,

kilo baskets of bleeding
    fruit. Ten thousand
zlotys to the dollar.

And all the presents
    that my parents brought
from Paris, West Berlin—

dolls in national
    costume standing quiet
on their metal stands, whole

girls cast in miniature,
    articulated joints,
each bisque mouth seamed shut—

a glittering answer
    to absence, which filled
the bookshelves in my room.

Each shopping bag
        was an opening,
each opening a bag,

our hands always reaching
     through the crisp whisper
of tissue paper

to pairs of cashmere socks,
     chocolate truffles
in their padded, velvet box.

As Seen on TV

To be On Sale among the merchandise.
To AutoVac. To Turbo Fricassee.
To Flexx and Sex and Silicone. To Ice
the shoulder when it hurts, to be pain-free
at last. To be a 2-for-1, a deal,
a steal, the One-Time Offer just today.
To be Smart Abs, CLICK HERE. To be the Real
McCoy, not sold in stores so Don't Delay.
Go Slenderize to Slim your arms and thighs.
A Super Home Alert to Save Your Life.
A Chippy Chopper Bloc to Pulverize
your onions in a flash. Your Ginsu Knife.
Your Back Relief. Your Better Baker Bowl.
Your fries, your chips, your Perfect Donut Hole.

YouTube—Tornado Throws a Bus

This isn't Kansas but southern Poland, and the sky is green as dollar bills, a bus idling beside what could be any country road in any country, folded-over trees, sick grass of summer, small houses at the vanishing, while the camera records air that bends at speeds increasingly malevolent, rounding toward the people in the bus, who shout Quiet and There, In Front of Us, then scream Jesus in the vocative, Jesu Jesu Jesu, too late of course, too late, because in a place historically too flat to halt armies as they churn up dirt, thresh fields with boots or the treads of armored tanks, what can stop this American import, this wind which makes amnesia of the landscape, wiping everything away, the horizon turning on its side, the bus tipped like a shot glass on a table, bodies tumbling at seats and windows, before the world goes pixelated, black.

Before Pleasure

Q: A Polish soldier has to choose between killing a
   Russian or a German soldier. Which does he shoot first?
A: He kills the German first—business before pleasure.

—COMMUNIST-ERA JOKE

We trafficked
in the oldest jokes
like a conversation everybody knew—
Where do you find
the finest view in Warsaw?
Why do police patrol in groups of three?
Something about
how many bureaucrats
it takes to screw a lightbulb in. Something
about democracy.
We were experts in the conditional:
if June then cherries in a paper bag.
So much was out
of reach. Not just the blonde
who shimmied on the naked stage
we called America,
not just the shopping mall
of her skin, but even the idea of her
was blue jeans
stacked on a shelf too high to touch.
Knock knock, we said, tapping the window
of the store
that closed ten years ago,
that trick of glass, transparent and impassable.